Carcharhinus obscurus

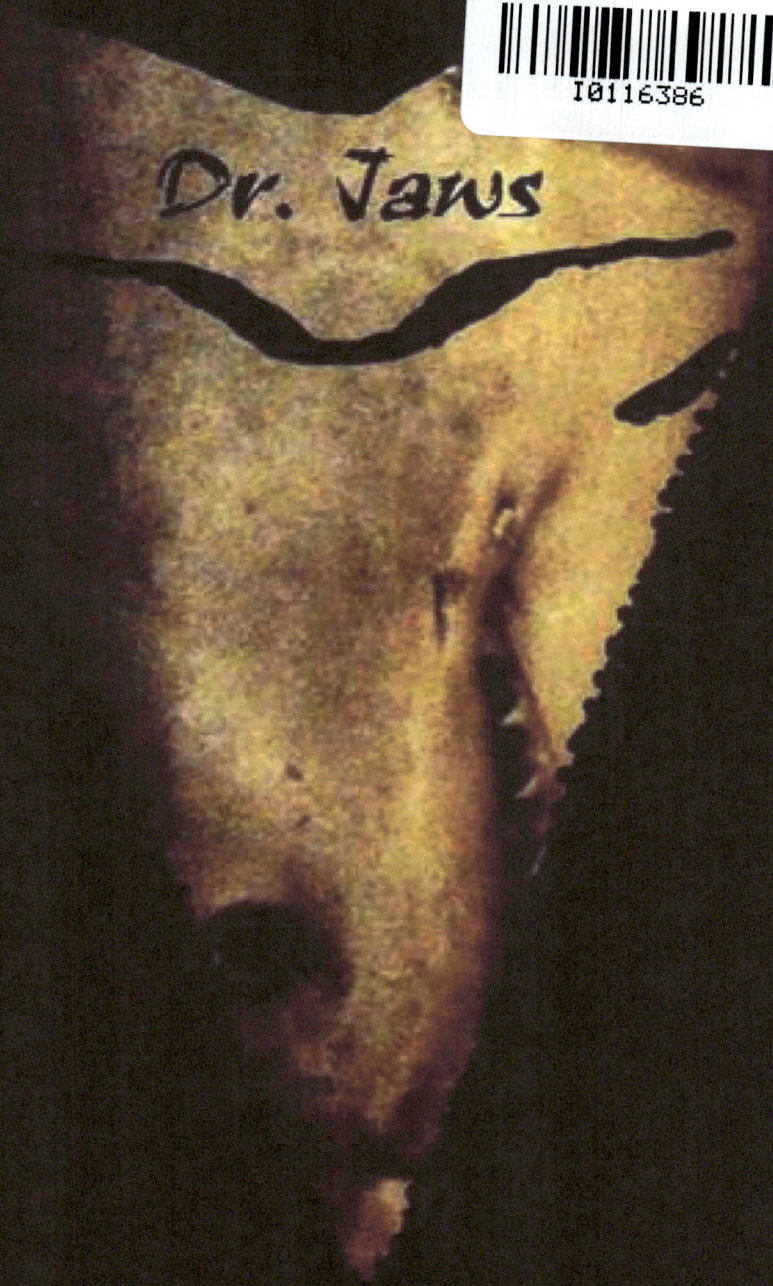

Dr. Jaws

Carcharhinus obscurus

Copyright © 2013 by Zachary Webb Nicholls

ISBN-13: 978-1-939535-16-0
ISBN: 1939535166
E-Book ISBN-13: 978-1-939535-17-7
E-Book ISBN: 1939535174

www.deepseapublishing.com

Printed in the United States of America

Hello friend,

What you are about to read is secret.

Each word, picture, and symbol has a meaning, and together they will help you find something very strange, but very exciting. Furthermore, each word, picture, and symbol is anchored in a living truth, but in order to fully understand what that truth is, you need to do some exploring.

Beyond this little book, there is a boundless, bountiful wealth of knowledge within your reach. You of course are not required to seek it, but if you do, I assure you will be rewarded with a richer understanding of our shark, the seas, and the mystery of life itself.

For now, you hold in your hands a map. Let it take you—from the past, to the present, to the weird—deep into an ocean of legends, of dark wonders, and of amber eyes…

.…let it take you to Shark.

Carcharhinus obscurus

Night is where you found me

And night is what I wear

Into the darkness your mind ascends

Or so you think

For I too bask in sunlight

And I too breathe and burn

The fires that I feast upon

Blood, I do not drink

Starlight is finite
A star has a time to end
Explosive its death

Scattered star pieces
Combine into the combined
Birth of sun and earth

Sun fire creates
With calm earth, air, and
water
Life elemental

~ *Domain Eukarya* ~

Imagine a mountain

Cool and calming

Trickling water down its slope

It is serene in its grey

Paint it with a domain

Of life so rich in color

That the eyes will forever wonder

At its design and sustain

A curiosity

Unique only to Eukarya

When cell within cell became cell itself

So long ago, a peak

In life was reached

From origins so humble

Came oranges so fiery

With jades, emeralds, and harlequins each

Beauties of the forest

Protecting the ambling reds

And boisterous blues

With calming arms best

Suited for shading

Amber-centered violets

And cinnabar-sighted mosaics

All art never fading

This domain is of color

See Eukarya

Splendid and diverse

Muses of the world

For the art that it is

~*Kingdom Animalia*~

Look what the dawn has broken

Something new stirs in the seas

A novel language now spoken

The animals have come to be

~

From one tiny sponge to one funny man

A simple life will always be banned

A drama that we cannot understand

The animals, come and play, come and play

A hardworking ant meets an unfriendly beetle

While two birds romance, it seems nothing's

sweeter

A seahorse's dance is such a unique love

Animals, come and play, come and play

~

Embrace the feeling of life

A body that's one from many

A hunger that sets you right

~

And chase in manner uncanny

Your strange sweet compassions

You animal, go and play, go and play

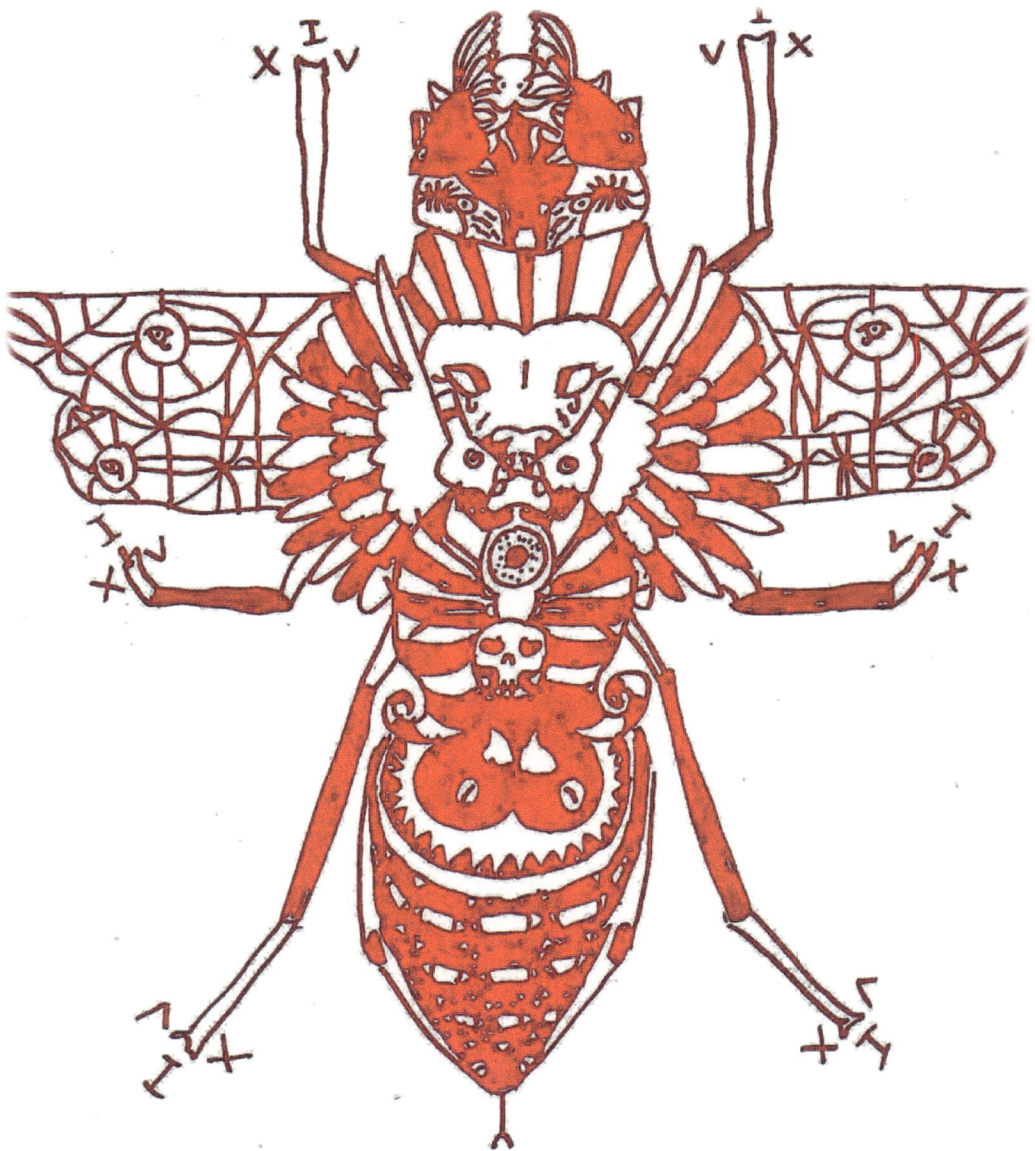

~Phylum Chordata~

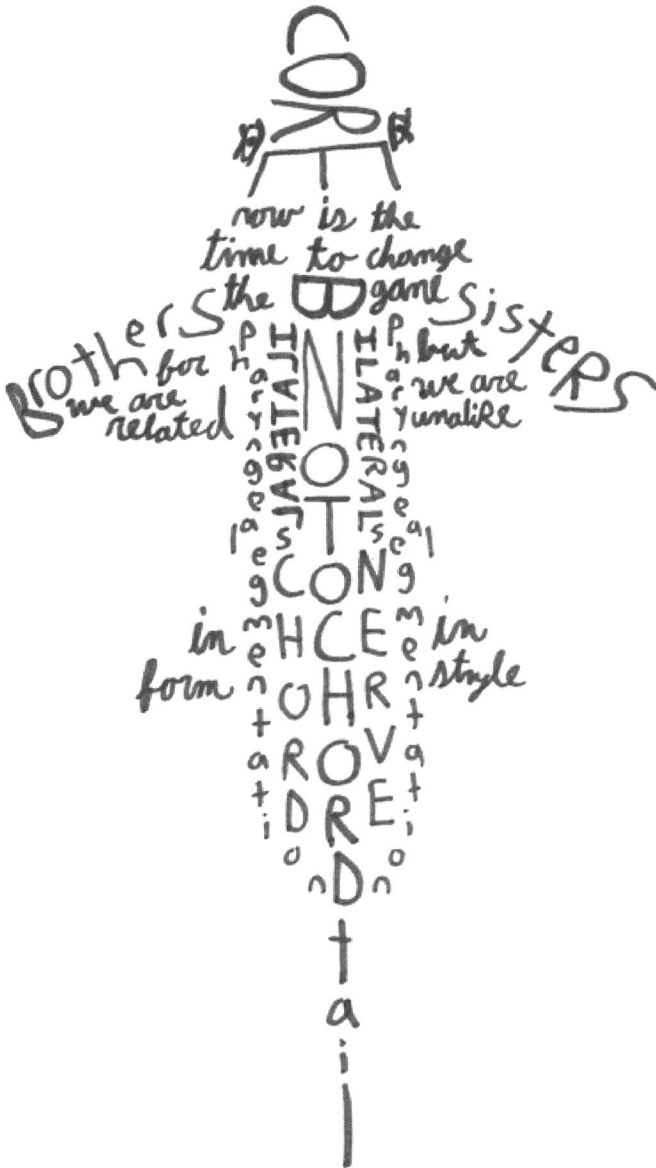

CORE

now is the
time to change
the game sisters

Brothers
for
we are
related

but
we are
you alike

PHARYNGEAL SLITS

BILATERALS

NOTOCHORD

CONVERGED

in form   in style

mentation   mentation

tail

~ *Class Chondrichthyes* ~

There is a hall of marble and limestone—of honor and ocean—adorned with obsidian shadows; the Chondrichthyan Silhouettes. Each Silhouette is an embodiment of form and essence, said to be constructed by the gods to remind the world of the Living Shadows; the chimaera, the ray, and the shark.

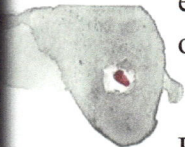

Believed to be guardians of both the ocean and the human soul, The Living Shadows served to consume the weaknesses of each. Through so doing, they culled corruption and protected the life of both soul and sea.

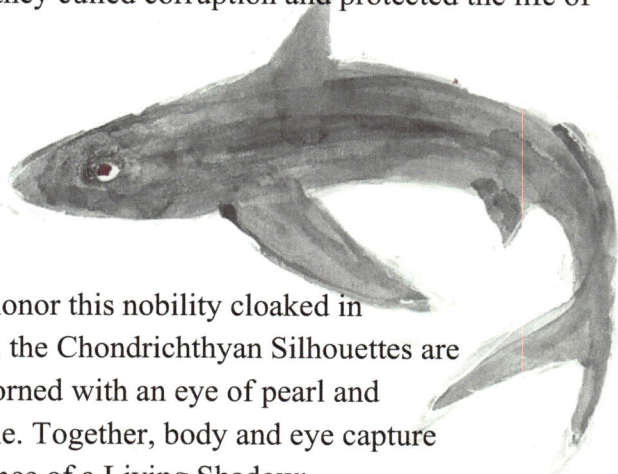

To honor this nobility cloaked in ferocity, the Chondrichthyan Silhouettes are each adorned with an eye of pearl and gemstone. Together, body and eye capture the essence of a Living Shadow:

A power cooled with grace
An immortal who could die
A legend with a heartbeat.

~Order Carcharhiniformes~

Beauteous beasts of time
A standard and yet an ideal
Coasting beyond the sands
And into depths of teal

For fear they do not
As in their eyes reveal
An ancient secret light
Seen only by those who feel

Akin to their plight
And akin to their strength
A cutting edge of blue
A coursing blood of length

By such eyes as theirs

Which close upon a kill

They form their sacred forms

The fears that we've instilled

These rare and common types

Of shark will always be

As changing as the tides

But still masters of the sea

~Family Carcharhinidae~

The requiem sharks
Aqua volcanoes aware
Powerful but calm

~*Genus Carcharhinus*~

SHARPNOSE

"Qcrpr d skjpduro qk er qcr 'pqljulou pclogp'; qcry lor ikpq djqroqwdjru wdqc ctiljdqy, lju lor qcr pqtaa ka hrbrjup"

Note: The above is a keyword cypher. The keyword is hidden on the following page. Use it to unlock a smaller insight.

The Dark One

Lesueur, 1818

Carcharhinus obscurus

A medium-sized shark, with an average mass of 170kg. It is distinguished by the placement of its 1st dorsal fin, which origi-nates above the free rear tip of its pectoral fin.

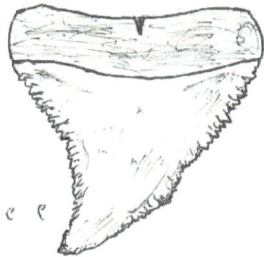

Dusky shark   Tiburón arenero

سانولی شارک   灰色真鲨   ドタブカ

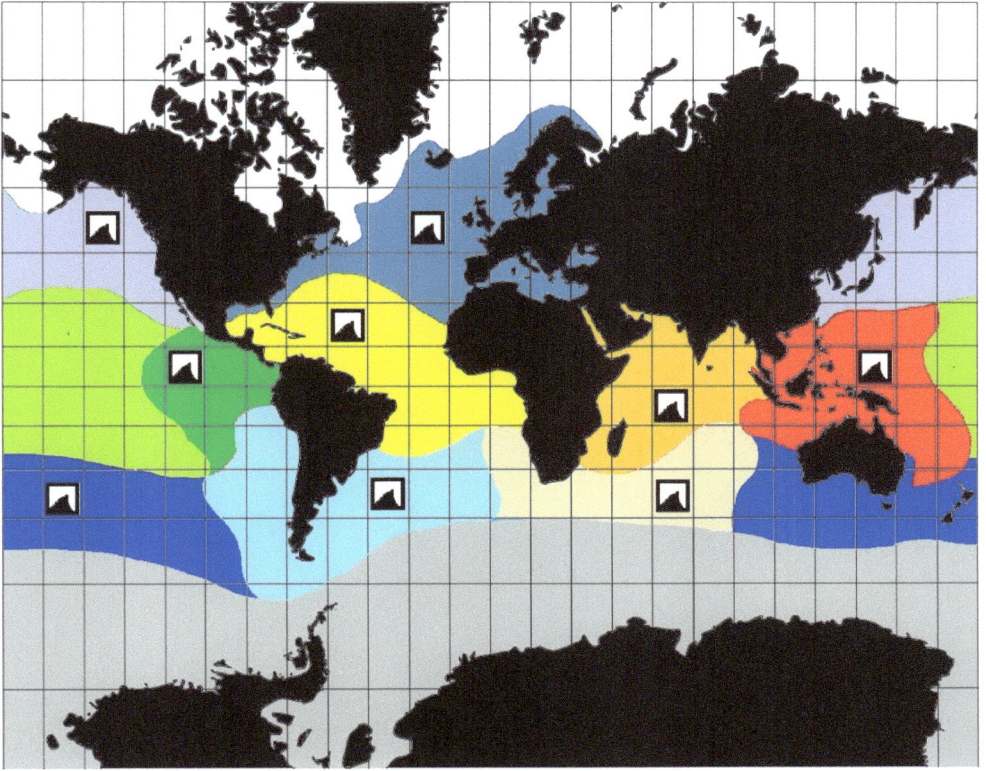

~Global Distribution~

North Akula Sea

Tempest Requin Sea

Wild Zame Sea

Sunset Sea of Reken

Colorful Sea of Sarka

Bountiful Sea of Shayu

Peaceful Sea of Mano

Sunrise Sea of Tiburon

Grande Tubarao Sea

Groot Haai Sea

Great Shark Sea

South Sarko Sea

~Haunts~

Carcharhinus obscurus

can be found in the following zones:

LITTORAL   NERITIC

OCEANIC   SUNLIT

TWILIGHT

~

"Deep, not abyssal, but deep nonetheless, big water, open sky, I ride the ocean waves but return to shore to hunt and play before the sun sets or when the sun rises it does not matter to me I still play amongst the waves, see the clouds, feel the bottom of the shelf and breathe clean open water, smell the salt and surf but submerge to the dark where I blend rather nicely but still wish to come up and feel the sun for I am ubiquitous, unchoosy, but happy"

~ *Habits* ~

Carcharhinus obscurus pups enter the world via live birth. When young, they enjoy shallow nursery areas along the coast. They are not picky eaters.

Adults undertake great journeys, coursing through the ocean by the whim of a changing sun. They live for a long time—purportedly up to 35 years—and mature late in life. *Carcharhinus obscurus* has one of the slowest rates of reproduction among animals due to its complex (and not fully understood) timing of gestation and birth.

~ *Humanity* ~

Carcharhinus obscurus is to be perceived as a

POTENTIALLY DANGEROUS SHARK

In light of the concerning attributes that follow;

Its considerable size

Its fearsome dentition

Its proximity to man

These attributes are juxtaposed with the truth that

Carcharhinus obscurus has been implicated in

VERY FEW UNPROVOKED ATTACKS

As a resource, the shark offers palatable meat, leather, and nutritious oil.

~

However, man has overfished Carcharhinus obscurus, and furthermore subjected the shark to the cruelty of finning.

As a result, Carcharhinus obscurus is a

VULNERABLE SPECIES

~ Sea of Sauda ~

"A tale about our shark, and more…"

He was feeling through a dark ocean...

Heavy was his mind, struggling to support a sense of calm as a behemoth of a wave seized his shell and threw him upward towards a sky of extinguished stars. How small he was. How insignificant his strength came to be. For though he was a powerful swimmer despite his age, he knew nothing of navigating through a typhoon.

To his deepest misfortune, the leatherback collided unexpectedly into an unnatural storm. Awesome were its black peaks of water, scraping a shrieking sky pierced with the berserk of lightning. In a calmer mindset, he would have appreciated its beauty, especially when the lightning ignited the South African waters into an electric blue.

Instead, the fact that he was a mortal in a titan's clench was extremely apparent. The thunder scared him. The winds ripped across his back. The waves subdued him and he had no control. But that was not the worst of it.

What most terrified him were the drums.

When he was small, the leatherback heard tell of their music and what it meant in this particular part of the ocean. Drums would play only for a Sea of Sauda; a condition in which a storm is at its most violent, death is at its most eminent, and *she* is at her most manifest.

At first he heard an agogo, but amongst the violence around him it did not register. Its music, however, intensified, and became accompanied by slit drums. Again, he was not convinced.

But when the djembes came, he realized in horror that the music was alive. Worse still, it was growing…

The drums got louder.

The storm was being tuned out.

The drums got louder.

The water was becoming ink.

The drums got louder.

A bass drum exploded into his ears, pulsating like a heartbeat.

It was all too much.

The insatiable noise would not stop until she broke the surface.

It was all too much.

She was coming…

STOP

From the peak of the highest swell the turtle descended, and as he did a sharp, black fin cut the tortured slope not too far away. He could not outswim her, for try as he might she would perfectly match his pace.

The noise, however, was gone. All that was around him was silenced, and now did not matter. He was alone, save for the wraith that shadowed him.

What now?

They arrived at the lowest trough. Strangely enough, the sea seemed to be calmed, though not to an extent that would bring the leatherback real comfort. She was encircling him.

'Perhaps I will die', he thought. He became sad, and yet curiously focused…

Perhaps you will not

Sauda spoke. The turtle was taken aback— he did not expect a reply.

'How can you hear me?'

No answer.

He stopped swimming. 'There is nothing I can do', he reasoned, 'if death is here then death will come. There is no escape.'

No escape

Again, the turtle was surprised. But this time it was the tone of her reply that struck him as shocking. It was distant still, yes, but somehow…amused?

"Are you mocking me?", he asked.

No answer.

"I understand", he began, "that in certain situations the finality becomes evident. In here, I have no chance of survival, and so I accept my fate. Thinking otherwise would be foolish, especially when considering the fact that she who puts me in danger is none other than Sauda… the guardian of the dead."

She did not respond.

He continued, this time in a more irate manner, "I believe my complicity to be wise, and as such I would expect it to be received in respect. Anything else I would perceive as torture…it is no secret that I am afraid, and my fears will only be amplified if my situation is mocked or, even more regrettably, prolonged."

A wave of sadness now tempered him.

"If you are indeed here to kill me, do so at once. Please do not continue my suffering. Please frighten me no more".

His eyes closed. He listened to his heartbeat—every small and precious pulse—perhaps for the last time.

Why so afraid?

This time it was he who did not reply.

There is truly nothing to fear.

He kept his eyes shut.

Especially if I do not kill you.

The tiny spark of hope spat forth by these words did nothing to move the leatherback, but he opened his eyes.

"What then is your purpose?"

Hidden.

"Why?"

All purposes are.

How helpful. He was too drained to press on further…he let his cares wander…

Must death really garner such sadness?

"You are currently not in death's grip", he retorted.

Yes I am. We all are.

"Well then I find my pessimism justified."

You forget, little turtle, that death is what defines life. Without it, what would you be? Why would you breathe, or eat, or sleep, or mate? Death is your contrast; it is the darkness that makes life your light.

"Well that's splendid then," he replied unmoved, "except for the likely chance of my soul being smote out within the hour."

Your soul will be fine. Your body will be mine.

These last words pierced down his spine and chilled him.

You mustn't be so afraid.

"And why not? Do you know what lies beyond?"

Do you?
"No. I don't know. No one knows, and that's the terrifying matter at hand."

A long silence followed. She was still circling him…calmly…gracefully…and it was now astounding to the leatherback that he saw beauty in his captor. She was dark, commanding…but young? How could she have such composure, in movement, in thought? She defied the waves, yet the water caressed her. Her eyes broke the darkness, but they blossomed from a heart of dusk.

Who was she?

Sauda suddenly became excited, and her circles were faster.

Guess.

Guess? Guess what? He voiced his question.

Guess that which is after death.

"Well…", the turtle began, only he didn't go very far in thought. He realized then and there how little he actually pondered about the afterlife itself. Of course, the event of death in concept danced around his mind often…but beyond…incredibly, he truly never gave deep consideration. Now was his time to try.

"Well…", he began again, more slowly, "I believe that the worst thing that could happen is something torturous…a punishment…a hell."

Are you to be punished?

He paused again, for a very long time. He looked at the waves around him, and noticed for the first time that he had been in a sort of perpetual trough; lightning and walls of water were waltzing around him, but his part of the sea was safe. He was protected.

"I don't believe so. I can't think of a reason why, as I have been of proper conduct. Furthermore, if I was unjustly punished, what purpose would that serve?"

You cite a sense of order.

"Well…I have order; I have two eyes, two ears, I am not allowed to fly…I cannot spout lightning"—the last he added amusedly—"so at the very least there is a natural order?"

She didn't reply.

The turtle then became himself excited, and asked in deep curiosity, "What brings this order? Who could be the punisher?"

Keep guessing.

Her tone of thought here changed subtly, but its meaning was drastic: she will not answer his question, and if he pressed further he felt for sure that he would become bitten in two. She was neither angry, nor afraid…she just became stronger.

"What about nothing?", he postulated, a bit more hesitantly. "There could very well be just…nothing. No air, no excitement, no food…just nothing."

Is that a problem?

"Of course it is."

Are you sure? Eternal slumber may be nice.

Eternal slumber. Eternal night. For the party slumbering, perhaps it wouldn't be that unpleasant. After all, living slumber is very comfortable. On this point, his spirits lightened, and he remained silent for a while.

What about rebirth?

He did not consider that; beginning life anew…but how? Why? What would he be? Another leatherback? Or something more basal…more impressive…a sponge…a shark.

"Is that what will happen?"

The minute he spoke these words he regretted them…what exactly *is* she doing? What is her game? The thought began to disturb him…Sauda is here to kill him. What comfort she had now brought became meaningless. "You toy with me."

That fearsome strength returned and she circled faster.

Make your final guess.

At that instant a small patch of sky was exposed, and the turtle looked up. Within this small circle surrounded by darkness and might, he saw the calmest moonlight surrounded by legions of the brightest stars. Together—star, moon, and midnight—they formed something that he could not comprehend, and had no words for…save for two.

"What souls…", he whispered.

It didn't make sense, but to him it was everything. How they danced. How he wish he could too…

"Heaven", he spoke loudly, composing himself. "There could be a heaven."

And then it began.

In a flash of lightning the skies closed and the drums returned…Sauda was on the move.

Night is where you found me…

She circled him, and so did the violent waters. Her eyes glowed, and her teeth were bared.

And night is what I wear…

Black, inky streaks started to appear and swirl about him. The leatherback was bewildered, and became once again terrified.

"WHAT ARE YOU DOING?", he shouted, but his voice didn't carry far.

Into the darkness your mind ascends…

Her voice was as clear as ice.

Or so you think.

The waters went mad. A ballistic ball of waves and thunder started to encase him. She was outside.

For I too bask in sunlight…

A hole emerged, and there she was. He stared down a gigantic shark, charging him with unbelievable speed. He shut his eyes.

And I too breathe and burn…

The hole closed, and he looked around. All was chaos, and the streaks turned brilliant red. He was searching madly all around him. No escape. A fin cut one side of the watery sphere in a flash.

The noise around him was unbelievable.

The fin cut again on the opposite side.

No escape.

The fires that I feast upon…

In a final flash of lightning, she broke inside the ball, her target locked.

Nothing stopped her.

Nothing could.

The final bite.

Blood I do not drink.

He awakened. Blue. Or turquoise? Some sort of tropical blue. The sky was clear. All was calm.

Where was he?

'I can't remember…there was a storm…but it was so long ago…Sauda…'

He looked around, but there was nothing in sight. Below was a white, sandy bottom with playful light dancing to the waves. He looked up and saw a brighter blue.

'Nice sky…calm winds…'

He came to the surface and looked around. An island lay behind him.

'What's that?', he thought.

It didn't look extraordinary.

'I think I'll try for it. Maybe there's something…so calm…I can't remember.'

"I think I'll try for that island.", he said aloud. He didn't care who heard him, but there seemed to be no one around.

Where was he?

'…Sauda.'

Respect the seas and all who call them home.

~ About the Author ~

photo by Van Kurt

"To my parents, Louis and Shawn Nicholls, thank you for your endless care, support, hardship, and love. Without any of these, I could not be who I am.

To Andy Murch, who possesses a plethora of powerful photos at Elasmodiver.com; thank you for that stunning shot of Carcharhinus obscurus. It made all the difference.

To those who may be inspired, never trade your inspiration. You can be whomever you want; that choice is always yours. Keep seeking your higher being, and never let go of your love. " ~Zachary Nicholls,

the First Dr. Jaws